Fascism for th

by

Oswald Mosley

Fascism for the Million
by
Oswald Mosley

ISBN-13: 978-1-908476-67-8

Black House Publishing Ltd

78 York Street

London

W1H 1DP

www.blackhousepublishing.co.uk
Email: info@blackhousepublishing.co.uk

The Golden Rule of Fascism

This is the Golden Rule of Fascism: All problems must be approached with the aim of putting the interests of

BRITAIN FIRST

After Britain, we put the interests of the Empire. Where there is a conflict of interest, whatever is best for the British people must prevail.

All sectional interests must be subordinated to the national interest; no one section must use its power for its own selfish purpose.

The Fascist State in Britain will come into existence in an orderly, legal, and constitutional manner.

The British Union of Fascists will attain power through the present electoral machine. Only when the people of Britain have, by a majority poll, declared their enthusiastic assent, will the British Union of Fascists commence the task of creating a Greater Britain.

We do not contemplate marching down Whitehall and seizing authority by force of arms, or forcibly turning members of Parliament out of their seats.

We wear uniforms but we are unarmed and will continue to be unarmed, for we desire to win our victory at the ballot box. If we do not, then we remain out of effective politics.

The present Parliamentary system will come to an end under Fascism, but as Sir Oswald Mosley has stated, we have first to capture Parliament before we can abolish the archaic system on which it rests.

It is hoped that the progress of the new Fascist State will be ordered and peaceful. There are some who believe that, as the power of Fascism increases, disorder will be provoked by the Trades Union Congress who will call, so it is said, a General Strike. This view ignores two important factors. First, the Unions will have a far more important role in the Fascist State than they have at present. Second, even Trade Union leaders have the good sense to know that an attempt to defeat the declared will of the people at a General Election, on a specific issue, will make them decidedly unpopular and will result in sharp and certain defeat.

Others believe that financial and newspaper interests will attempt, in conjunction with Tory reactionaries, and assisted by officers of the Army and Navy, a coup d'etat. This fear, too, is groundless.

By the time we are strong enough to win a General Election we shall possess a Press more powerful than the present anti-Fascist Press, and the Army and Navy will accept our constitutional and legal claims, especially as we are intensely loyal to the Monarchy.

As the Fascist Government proceeds to put its plans into operation, however, trouble may develop from financiers, particularly those of alien origin. They may attempt to create a panic. They will not succeed, for the Fascist Government will be in control of all propaganda within the State, and, with the aid of the Fascist Press, will easily be able to counteract their influence.

Immediate deportation of undesirables is a weapon that can be employed against unscrupulous foreign financiers. But repressive measures will not be adopted by Fascists unless hostility is forthcoming from their opponents. The opponents, however, will be in a minority, and, though powerful, will be required to put the interests of the majority of the people before their own interests.

When the Blackshirts have won power at a General Election, Sir Oswald Mosley, the Leader of the British Union of Fascists, armed with the authority bestowed upon him by the King, will proceed to create his Government and to form a Corporate State.

Fascism in Britain has for its main purposes the complete banishment of every form of poverty, with all its symptoms of slums, hunger, filth and disease. Hunger is the first evil to be attacked. No spiritual life can thrive under the duress of involuntary hunger; and there can be little that is fine in manhood or womanhood when human beings are herded in hovels like vermin, and when many of their dwelling places are below ground, liable to be flooded by filthy river water, or by the inky streams and canals that run through our industrial towns of the North. Slumdom kills the spirituality of mankind just as effectually as it stupefies mental capacity and stultifies the body.

Spiritual development is essential and no nation can exist without it, but the stomach not only enables an army to march, but also a nation to live. Fascists demand that the people should be well fed and housed, well clothed, and should possess all reasonable means of enjoyment. Fascists demand that the people should have the opportunity to enjoy, if they so desire, fine music, great libraries, all forms of sport, and all the essentials to live a fully adequate life.

These gifts are to be had if the people will demand the power to possess them. If the present organisation had succeeded in feeding the people and in giving them the things which are essential to happiness, then it would have continued to exist. Man will go on experimenting and improving social organisation, either in this or in some other country, until he has brought it to perfection. It is because the present system has failed that new movements arise, that men turn to Socialism, Communism, or Fascism. The system that gives the people what they desire must prevail. If Fascism does not succeed in delivering at least this minimum demand, then sooner or later it will die a natural death.

If it declines to die naturally, there are many who will see that it dies unnaturally, and they will be justified. No system can live, or has the right to live, unless it is a success.

1 - How Fascism Came to Britain

The public of this country know of Fascism only from what they read in some sections of the popular press and from the vapourings of hostile street corner propagandists. Many regard Fascists as "thugs" and reactionaries of the worst type. When a Government department appoints a Commissioner to administer a "means test" harshly—that is called, quite wrongly, Fascism! When Lord Trenchard puts police officers into boiled shirts—that, too, is said to be Fascism! When some Tory propounds national aggrandise ment and pressure on an obscure part of the Empire, that is called Fascism!

The public, of course, cannot be blamed. While they regard the greater part of the daily Press as a daily joke, they still believe that there must be some substance in the continuous abuse of Fascism.

Violence a Product of Revolution

Barbarities and cruelties, in point of fact, are associated with all violent revolutions and are not products of Fascism. Communism in Russia used every method of violence imaginable to achieve power and to maintain it; the French Revolutions were the most bloodthirsty ever recorded. Yet nobody could say that Lenin and Trotsky were Fascists, or that Robespierre wore a black shirt. Revolution breeds violence, and as Macaulay and Carlyle have pointed out in their studies of history, the more corrupt and reactionary the preceding condition, the more violent the revolution.

Violence, therefore, is a characteristic of revolution, and not of any one particular school of politics. Historical proof of this is to be found in the violence that accompanied the demand for franchise in this country in the early part of the last century, in the Communistic movement of Russia, the anarchist movements of Spain, and in the Fascist uprisings on the Continent. When ever men become desperate they become violent. Masses of men, women and children wanting bread and shelter, fuel and clothing, and denied these things, become desperate. They become like animals hungry in the jungle, and will fight with all the cruelty of starving beasts. They rise in their hunger and their anger and smite down those whom they believe to be their oppressors. The innocent suffer with the guilty. Justice and mercy are discarded in the cruel determination to put an end to oppression. This is true of every revolutionary outbreak.

It is no use endeavouring to apply ordinary standards when judging hungry men and women. The Chartists of this country a hundred years ago; the men of the north who rebelled when thrown into the streets by the advent of machinery; the mobs of Paris, of Moscow, Rome, and Berlin can all perhaps be condemned in the light of cold reason—but cold reason is a quality not to be found among desperate peoples.

Fascism, therefore, does not lead to violence. What does terminate in violence is the attempt to patch up a decaying system which cannot be patched up.

Fascism Will Prevent Economic Collapse

Fascism in this country, it cannot be too often repeated, will achieve power by constitutional, legal, and orderly means. Britain has the advantage of being able to decide for herself what her future economic organisation will be. Other countries had to adopt Fascist principles owing to a breakdown of a previous system—or lack of system. They had not time to choose. Italy especially, adopted Fascism as a rapid means of extricating the country from a threat of complete breakdown.

If disaster does overtake the country, Fascists will intervene to prevent chaos. Unfortunately the Communists are waiting for that day of collapse as well, and if it should come they will attempt to seize power for themselves. The struggle will then be between Fascists and Communists.

Today Fascists urge that such a disaster should not be allowed to occur. We appeal to our countrymen to save this land from the untold horrors of severe economic dis location and civil war, from the agonising spectacle of millions of men, women and children starving and roaming the streets in search of food.

Fascism will enable Britain to avoid such degradation and will create for our country a higher civilisation than it has yet known.

UNITY IS STRENGTH

The term "Fascism" originated in Italy, where Signor Mussolini created his "Blackshirts" shortly after the war. The badge they wore was the ancient Roman symbol of unity. The main part of it represented the "fasces" bound together. Singly, each one could be snapped, but bound together, they were unbreakable. Applying it to the National life, the symbol has real significance. If all the sections that make up a country's population are separated, they can be broken, but a nation united is a nation unbreakable. This is particularly true in an economic sense. If the constituent parts of industry, such as the employers and the workers, are always engaged in ruinous stoppages of work, whether described as "lockouts" or strikes, then industry also will be ruined, but if the warring sections work together, then industry is stronger and more profitable for both.

The axe at the head of the "fasces" signifies the determination to cut out the rot of national life. That such rot exists no one denies, but only Fascists are determined to cut it out and remove it.

This badge has been adopted by the British Union of Fascists. The "fasces," as an emblem of corporate municipal life, has long been associated with the high ideals of public service in Britain, and it is a common heritage of Britain and other countries from the Roman Empire of which we once formed a part.

Attitude to Jewry

Many people associate Fascism in Britain with Fascism in Italy, and also with the National Socialist Movement in Germany, and it is true that Fascism is a world-wide creed, but in each country it finds an application in keeping with the traditions of the country that has adopted it.

The National Socialists of Germany and the Fascists of Italy differ in many important respects. For example, there has been no persecution of the Jews in Italy, and Jews hold high positions in that country. But in Germany, as the world knows, many Jews have been the object of discrimination. The British Union of Fascists, when it comes to power will treat Jews and Gentile on their merits. Both will be under the same law, and both will be called upon to put the welfare of the nation before any sectional or racial interest.

We believe, however, that many of the economic and financial ills from which we suffer as a people are due to the ownership of capital by Jews. In commerce, the Jews possess a low standard of morals. They are greedy, selfish and unscrupulous; they operate internationally to gain control over the lives of each nation; and they exploit the working classes by cut-throat wages, and bad conditions. All the trades and industries in which conditions are bad, are controlled either directly or indirectly by Jews.

Jews will be compelled by Fascism to cease applying their low code of morality to the commercial, financial and social life of the country.

Why We Wear Black Shirts

We wear black shirts for several reasons. When all members are dressed similarly, social status and class are forgotten, together with all the other shams of modern civilisation: and we remember only that we are embarked on a common cause, that we recognise no artificial distinctions, and above all that we have no hatred for those whom fate has thrown in a different sphere.

This does not mean that we are so foolish as to imagine that all men are equal. Some possess talents that others have not, but Fascists insist that whether a man is styled a labourer, a skilled worker, a technician, or a "professional," all men and all women have a fundamental right to a place in society. All that Fascists ask is that those to whom these rights are accorded, should, in return, be prepared to further the interests of society as a whole, and not their own sectional interests.

Another reason why black shirts are worn is that they enable one Fascist easily to recognise another. Frequently Fascist meetings have been attacked by Communists and in the melee that has resulted, Fascists properly uniformed, disciplined, and trained in the art of self-defence, are in a more advantageous position for defending themselves against aggression.

In passing, it can be said with absolute truth that Fascists have never attempted to interfere with political meetings organised by Conservative, Labour, Liberal or Communist parties. Some of our opponents have endeavoured to prevent us from holding meetings and have attacked our speakers. On such occasions, our stewards, who are trained for the task, protect the speakers at indoor meetings and eject persistent interrupters in the same manner that they are ejected at political meetings of other parties.

THE EVCOLUTION OF FASCISM IN BRITAIN

The British Union of Fascists came into existence in October, 1932, when Sir Oswald Mosley, the Leader, published "Greater Britain." It is true that before that event there had existed other Fascist organisations, chiefly the British Fascists which recently became bankrupt, and the Imperial Fascist League. Neither of these organisations, however, had gained any numerical strength, and their influence on English public life was negligible. Their policy, if they had one at all, was of a reactionary character. The Tories, from their point of view, were not severe enough on the Socialists and Communists, and these so-called Fascists were anxious to create an organisation that was merely negative and anti-Socialist.

The British Union of Fascists, unlike these other organisations, came into existence on a definite constructive economic theory, evolved after the political experience of its Leader and those associated with him, in the years that elapsed from 1920 to 1931, a period in which the economic structure of Britain was badly shaken.

Fundamentally, the British Union of Fascists stands or falls by the validity of its economic reasoning and its economic proposals. If it is wrong in its economics then its efforts must result in failure. This does not mean that the British Union of Fascists is interested solely in industrial and economic problems. It is vitally concerned with the problems of the future government of India, the relationship between the constituent parts of the Empire, the activities of the League of Nations, and the development of the system of social services in Britain. But it also recognises that economic factors will decide the fate of modern civilisations and will level up, or down, all the social amenities that man has now become accustomed to regard as his inalienable right.

Sir Oswald Mosley was driven to examine Fascism almost against his will, though, as a matter of fact, he had reached conclusions similar to those embodied in the principles of the Italian Corporate State. It should not be forgotten that for many years the nature of the Italian experiment was not revealed to the British public. Mussolini, since acclaimed as one of the world's greatest statesmen, was daily subjected to vile epithets and sneers from the British Press. Either the newspapers of this country did not understand the character of Mussolini's activities — which is quite possible — or, under standing, failed to realise their significance — which is even more possible. Besides, there were many spicy murders to report, and at that period reports of divorce cases were not prohibited!

FAILURE OF THE OLD PARTIES

Sir Oswald Mosley entered politics at a very early age as a young officer of the Royal Air Force. His political record since 1918 is common knowledge. It is the subject of frequent taunts, how first he was an official Conservative, then an Independent Conservative; how later he became an important member of the Independent Labour Party, sitting on the Administrative Council, and, until, after a short experience with the Labour Party, he broke away to form the New Party and eventually the British Union of Fascists. As Mosley himself has stated, nobody can complain that he has not given the older political parties a fair trial!

MOSLEY IN A HURRY

Mosley, it is said, was far too impatient; he wanted things done in a hurry. That was a charge brought against him by his opponents, but it is a charge to which he should be proud to plead guilty. There is no crime in being in a hurry when unemployment is increasing by hundreds of thousands, as it was in 1930 and 1931. When men and women are being thrown out of the mines, mills and work shops, when destitution is stalking grim and determined over our land, where is the offence in asking that statesmen should regard the problem as one of extreme urgency?

The break with the Conservative Party that came early in Mosley's career is perfectly understandable. Perhaps Conservatives possess some merits, but energy is not one of them. They have had vast majorities since the days of the war, but they had not used their opportunities to devise a policy for dealing with economic breakdown, excepting that of the negative "safety first." No man who believed that civilisation had been through the melting pot of the war years and that a new philosophy and outlook on economic and national life was essential, could tolerate for long the Conservative Party.

Mosley's break with the Labour Party is even more under standable. The Labour Party had developed into a political force on Keir Hardie's cry of "Work or maintenance." This Party had a grim responsibility, direct to the working classes. Out of the pennies of the workers a huge political machine had been built. Men like MacDonald, Thomas, Snowden, Alexander, Greenwood, and others, had either been paid out of the coffers of working-class organisations or had gained notoriety by their political activities on behalf of working-class interests. They were, in fact, the servants of the workers, and owed to the masses of the country the debt of reconstructing the economic system whereby the workers should be provided with "Work or Maintenance."

Yet the Labour Party, when in office, forgot all that they had ever promised the working-classes and instead of carrying through or attempting to carry through, the revolutionary policy which they had previously proclaimed, floundered from one blunder to another.

A Revolutionary

Mosley had always been, and still is, a revolutionary. That was why he was popular with the rank and file of the Labour Movement. The workers thundered their applause at his meetings because they appreciated that he was a sincere revolutionary. His personal prestige, outside official circles, was immense and it was simply because the people who worked for their livelihood knew that here was a man who meant what he said.

When the Labour Party accepted office in 1929, there were signs in the outer regions of the world, particularly in Australia and in the South American Continent, of the coming economic storm. It was a storm that by 1929 was inevitable, owing to the financial policy that the world, and especially, Britain, had been pursuing. The return to the Gold Standard had created a heavy burden on industry all over the world, far greater than industry could bear. Australia made many mistakes in her financial and economic policy, but the error that caused her most trouble, and indeed, caused most troubles everywhere was that monetary policy created a greater drain on her industries than she could meet. Every financial burden became intensified. The world was rocking visibly under the strain.

Deflationary policy in this country had been sponsored by Winston Churchill and Philip Snowden, with the approval of both the Conservative and the Labour Parties, and between them they had given, as free gifts, colossal wealth to the rentier classes at the expense of all engaged in industry. The industrial situation in this country was rapidly deteriorating when Labour took office, and remembering the responsibility of his Party to the working-classes, Mr. Macdonald appointed four men to deal with the problem of unemployment, Mr. J. H. Thomas, Mr. George Lansbury, Mr. Tom Johnston and Sir Oswald Mosley.

Mosley took his job seriously—an error perhaps, judged from the point of view of a careerist, for nobody in official circles likes the man who takes his task seriously—and framed definite proposals for the solution of unemployment. These proposals, as everybody knows, were turned down, and Mosley did what every politician should do in such circumstances, he resigned his office. The Labour Party appeared unconcerned, but Mosley was strong in the favour of the ordinary members of the party in the country and he had a tumultuous reception at the Llandudno Conference.

Mosley, however, was soon to realise that the loyalty of the Labour members to the Labour Party machine was stronger than his personal popularity, and that if he desired to be effective, in the course of time he would have to break with a machine that was slow to move, and that was filled with personal jealousies and striving intrigues.

He took with him a few others into open rebellion to form the New Party. He knew, with the opposition of the official Labour Party machine against him that he would never succeed in getting the Labour Government to tackle the economic evils of the country in the vigorous manner that was essential.

The New Party

The New Party was unfortunate from the start. Sir Oswald himself was stricken down with pleurisy within a day or two of the formation of the party, and in his absence many decisions were reached, and many appointments were made to key positions, that were bad. The big flaw in the New Party policy, however, was that it fell between two stools. It boasted that it was not concerned with "isms," or with academic discussions on whether it was bolstering up capitalism, or was paving the way to socialism. It was intended as a policy to deal with the economic problems then existing and those immediately threatening. Mosley had seen that an economic storm was soon to burst over the country and he desired a policy of "insulation" against the worst effects.

When the General Election came in the autumn of 1931, the Party fared badly—but not too badly, in view of the intensified propaganda and the appeal of the National Government. None of the Party's twenty-three candidates was elected, but Sir Oswald Mosley polled over ten thousand votes at Stoke-on-Trent.

An effort to pull the Party together was made in the weeks after the Election, but the end had come. The New Party was to evolve within twelve months into the British Union of Fascists, and thereby to go forward at a greater pace towards its ultimate success.

Fascism Inevitable

The decision to come out bodily as a Fascist was not one that was undertaken lightly. Opposition to Fascism was uppermost in the minds of the British public as it was associated with thuggery and castor oil. But hardly any other decision was possible. The New Party policy, in point of fact, did not differ in its essentials from that of the British Union of Fascists, and when in the summer of 1931, New Party speakers were carrying on their propaganda work, they were alleged to be Fascists by their opponents. Mosley was dubbed another Hitler, and Communists everywhere made political activity for the New Party one of great difficulty, and in some parts of the country, of real danger. Mosley found it essential, even in those early days, to organise groups of men who could keep order at his meetings. One often hears it said that the Fascists are provocative and that appearing in a black shirt arouses the crowd to fury. Such charges cannot be substantiated for a moment, for in the days long before uniforms were worn, New Party speakers were assaulted violently and meetings were broken up.

The British Union of Fascists, therefore, was not formed in a careless moment. The decision was taken after a hard, bitter struggle to make the old political and social machine do its job, the task of providing for the masses a fair share of the goods they produced.

Mosley found, as a matter of fact, that neither Tory nor Labour possessed the slightest intention to alter the economic or Parliamentary machine, and, therefore, he broke with them, came out into the open, and declared emphatically that he intended to alter the whole political machine, to set up another in its place and that to do this he would have to forge a new political organisation.

2 - The New System of Government

The new machinery of government that Fascists intend to set up is described as the Corporate State.

By the Corporate State, Fascists mean an ordered system, working on the principles of co-operation and under the guidance of experts. Today, we contend, the economic life of the country is unplanned, that it is opportunist, that it lives from day to day and has no "long-term " policy : we intend to substitute a system in which government will not operate for any one class or section of the community, but for the whole; in which finance, and the whole organisation of manufacture and distribution will be marshalled and co ordinated to serve the end of the nation.

This Corporate State is the next stage in the evolution of industrial organism. The nineteenth century was the period of "free capitalism." Today we move on to the period of " controlled capitalism." Free capitalism was based on "laissez faire," the policy which is defined in the Encyclopaedia Britannica" as "the doctrine which demands the minimum interference by government in economic and political affairs." Laissez-faire, however, is dead, and Mr. J. M. Keynes, the noted Liberal economist, some years ago, wrote the obituary notice of this doctrine in a significant booklet "The End of Laissez-faire."

CONTROLLED CAPITALISM

This condition of "controlled capitalism," which we call the Corporate State, has as its main proposal the creation of Corporations for Industry and Finance. All production and distribution will be organised and controlled; nothing will be left to chance, and above all, nothing will be left to that stupidity known as economic warfare.

Organisation and team-work are the keynotes of Fascist policy, and both these ideas are in keeping with the best traditions of the British people, and are accepted in the every day life of the country.

Particularly do the British people understand the significance of team-work in relation to liberty. They like a brilliant individualist, but they hate a selfish individualist, no matter how brilliant he may be. Especially is this so in sport. The sporting public insist, and are quite right in insisting, that the individual must play with the team, and for the team. If he fails to do this, the British people will "boo" him off the field. Team work is insisted upon and no player has the "liberty" to play his own game, excepting in so far as the welfare of the team as a whole is concerned; otherwise, out he goes.

The principle of organisation and authority in sport is also fully accepted by "the man in the street." The British have developed sport on a definitely organised basis. They have created the Football Association, the Rugby Union, the Rugby League, and many other sporting organisations, all of which are exceedingly powerful bodies, exercising absolute control. The public realise that without these controlling organisations, sport as we know it today would be absolutely non-existent. And none of these organisations has false notions of "liberty." Every club and every member in alliance, membership or federation, has to obey the rules laid down from above.

At the same time, the members and clubs who are the constituent bodies of these controlling organisations have a definite voice on questions of policy and a definite part in drawing up the rules that have to be observed (and so will the members and organisations in the Fascist State) but no opposition with the object of holding up the work or stopping it altogether is tolerated for a moment.

A GENERAL STAFF FOR INDUSTRY

The machinery for controlling the general policy of industry and finance, of the equating of prices, the adjusting of working conditions, the remuneration of labour, and above all for providing industry with a direct route along which to travel and develop, will be centralised in a National Council of Industry—a Parliament of Industry representative of all sections of the community engaged in productivity, which will have the expert assistance of leaders of science, sociology, technicians, and accountants, elected by the individual Industrial Corporations. This Council will be in supreme charge of industrial policy and its decisions will have statutory effect. These will be enforced with the utmost rigour of law. If, for instance, it decides that a minimum wage is essential, such a wage will be legal and employers and employees who pay or accept a less rate will be guilty of punishable offences. Contrast this with the present system under which employers and trade unions make wage agreements which are more honoured in the breach than in the observance. Breaking the Fascist industrial law will mean expulsion from business.

The National Council of Industry will be the General Staff of Industry. Industry today is like an army without a leader. Its units are all at loggerheads; most of them want to do different things, often they do not know what to do next, and the result is that the units fall into disorder and, in the course of time, become broken up and demoralised. That is what has happened to industry, and what must continue to happen until it is organised on a Fascist basis. All that Fascism says is that industry must have leadership, must work to system, and must have a plan.

INDUSTRIAL CORPORATIONS

Each of the great industries of the country will be formed into Corporations which will lay down the limits within which private enterprise will be permitted to operate. They will aim at producing definite quantities of any given com modity, the fixation of minimum rates of wages, the ascertainment of fair charges for distribution and, finally, the merchanting of it at a fixed price. This method of pro duction and distribution is not so difficult as it might sound to the uninitiated. It relies on a supply of statistics that an expert body of accountants can produce with little trouble.

To take Agriculture as an example, all the statistical data is available. It is known exactly how much wheat, bacon, beef, mutton, butter, cheese, milk, etc., is required to feed the population of this country. It is known to a satisfactory approximation how much this country can produce with the present acreage in use, and how the quantity can be increased as the standard of living of the people became higher. In the event of this country being unable to meet its own require ments, it is known which of the Dominions can be relied upon to supply the deficiencies.

What is equally important is that the statistical organisation will work in close co-operation with the medical authorities, who will decide what people ought to be consuming in the way of essential food-stuffs; and productive capacity for the first time, would be related to the consuming public.

In the same way that the production of goods will be according to schedule, so will imports and exports. It will be impossible to allow traders of Britain to import and to export goods as they desire, for such freedom would ruin the "planned" economy.

REPRESENTATIONS OF ALL SECTIONS

Such Corporations, however, will fail to function if they do not inspire widespread confidence. They would be regarded as industrial autocrats, wielding tremendous executive powers. Sooner or later, faith in their ability would be destroyed if they had no direct contact with the rank and file of industry and were not representative of the sections within industry. Therefore each Corporation will be made up of the following:

1. Representatives of employers' organisations;
2. Representatives of trade unions and professional organisations;
3. Representatives of the consumers' interests.

It is obvious that no organisation of this character can be created unless every employer is a member of the employers' organisation and, also, unless every worker is a member of his (or her) trade union or professional organisation.

Within the general limits laid down by the National Council of Industry, each Industrial Corporation will be expected to function for the benefit of the majority of those whom it represents.

Progressive employers will welcome such an organisation, for in the past most of their efforts to improve their productive machinery have been held up by strongly individualist employers who have preferred to play their own game and have not cared if they ruined their fellow-manufacturers. There is a type of employer who repeatedly ignores all agree ment with trade unions regarding wages and conditions, in the same way as he disregards all agreements with other employers. He prefers to adopt a selfish policy because he thinks he can score a temporary advantage. It is this type of employer who has been a retarding factor in many schemes for the betterment of industry. Under Fascism, the view of the majority will prevail, and all employers will be bound by the code that their Corporation, of which they as members, have laid down, and the penalty of disobeying that code, will be, in the worst cases, expulsion from the industry.

This, however, is not a tyranny that the best employers will fear, for it goes no further than the established practice of important professions. Lawyers, for instance, are rigorously bound by a code laid down by the Law Council just in the same way as doctors are bound by the General Medical Council. In each case the profession benefits, as any profession or industry must benefit, whenever the individual puts the interests of his calling first, and not his own selfish gain.

Exactly the same system of organisation will be applicable to the workers, but the position of the working-classes under the

Corporate State and in the Industrial Corporations is dealt with at greater length in a subsequent chapter.

The successful representation of the consumers will not be so easy, but already there is a large body of consumers organised in the Co-operative Society movement. The Co-operative Society will find a definite place in the Fascist organisation and will become more what it was intended to be, that is, a general grouping of consumers to safeguard consumers' interests. The Co-operative Society movement, as a matter of fact, will find within a Fascist State an atmosphere for development far more healthy than that which exists today. The membership of these societies today is only nominal. The members join, shop at the branch stores and are content to draw the dividend. Over ninety per cent, of them rarely attend a meeting; they take no part in the framing of rules; they do not attempt to adjust policy and they certainly have no part in controlling prices. That is not real organisation of consumers; neither is it the exercise of power by consumers. In the Fascist State, the consumers will be encouraged to take an active interest in the management of the Co-operative Society, and through the Society, will have a voice in the direction of the industrial Corporations. The non-Co-operative consumer, too, will be invited and encouraged to take a real part in the operations of the governing body. This class of consumer, will, of course, deal with the private trader who for the first time will find a secure living in his shop. He will be free from the constant undermining of his business by the cut-price merchant; and will be relieved of the competition of the cheap chain-stores that now exist for the benefit of foreign financiers. Further, he will benefit enormously from the increased spending power that will be available to consumers, and he will find that though the gross profit on the individual commodities that he sells over the counter is not so large, his net profits will have a stability that they have lacked in the past.

The "consumers" of the products of the major industries will be far easier to organise and the manufacture of chemicals and dyestuffs can be mentioned as a typical example. Under a Fascist State, the control of the manufacture of chemicals and dyestuffs will be in the hands of a Corporation representative of the owners, the trade unions, and in this case, the Colour Users' Association and other users of the products of this industry. On the Corporation these three sections will operate, with a staff of the finest technical experts, for the benefit of the whole of the industry.

This is a bare outline of the machinery for governing industry under a Corporate State. Fascists claim that industry must be governed and this system of the Corporate State is the best that has been devised, because it provides for the representation of all sections, thereby ensuring the general confidence in its impartiality, and makes provision for an important place for the technician, without whom no industry can prosper. This Corporate control of industry is "government of industry by industry," and not government by Whitehall or Westminster. It is not nationalisation or socialism in any sense; it is entirely divorced from civil service influence but at the same time is a complete break with the old idea that industry should be left alone.

The distributive trades also must be properly organised. At present too much money goes into the pockets of the middlemen and travellers, in the way of commissions, and far too little to the producers. It is well-known that in some branches of industry the distributive costs exceed by six or seven times the cost of manufacturing the article. There must always, of course, be distributive costs, but at present these are far too excessive. Fascism will cut out the terrific wastage of commissions of the numerous middlemen, and will end the constant drain on industry that takes place today.

OCCUPATIONAL FRANCHISE

The creation of this chain of Industrial Corporations will mean a change in the whole system of representation of the people in the government of the country, and a new franchise qualification.

At present, every man and woman in the country, over the age of 21, who has been resident for a comparatively short period in one constituency, is entitled to cast a vote, every few years, for a Parliamentary representative. In addition, nearly all adults possess a periodical vote to elect representatives on the local governing authority.

Theoretically, it should have been a perfect system, but in practice, it has worked out with ludicrous results. In many constituencies, for instance, you will find a group of residential houses in one corner, agriculturists in another, and perhaps miners in a third, and at a general election they will have a choice of candidates, most probably a young Tory lawyer—and a trade union leader, neither of whom has a first-hand knowledge of the work and economic difficulties of the voters. There is no unity or community of interest between the voters. On the contrary, their economic interests may be, and quite often are, diametrically opposed, and they are called upon to choose between two candidates whose only claim to a vote is that they have by some means established themselves at the central offices of a political organisation in London.

By no stretch of the imagination can this be described as a sane system of electing the rulers of a great country like Britain; by no stretch of the imagination can it be called "government of the people, by the people, for the people." It is not surprising therefore, that in practice, it has broken down, and not since the war, has the expressed will of the people of Britain been carried out. The people have constantly beseeched their rulers to get on with the government of the country, to solve their economic and industrial problems, but their demands have been in vain.

Electioneering since the war has been a farce—just as much as it was in the old days when Tories used to go floating down to Westminster on barrels of beer. In fact, it is worse. In those days, the bribery and corruption that existed was open and free—today it is more subtle, more insidious. Instead of trying to bribe the elector with a glass of beer, the politician today bribes him with all sorts of promises, arouses his fears and prejudices, influences his mind with all manner of irrelevant considerations and the successful candidate is the one who best can use all the arts of flattery, bribery, cajolery, bullying and elocutionary frightfulness. Coupon elections, Khaki elections, Red Letter elections, Safety First elections—there has not been a general election of recent times that has not roused the disgust of even the electors themselves. The political parties of this country have performed a wicked disservice to the finer instincts of the British people—they have destroyed its love of being given a chance of selecting the best man.

Nobody believes statements made on either side in elections; but that is how elections are won—by lying propaganda and playing upon the fears of the electorate. Is this system worthy of this age? Is it a system that is likely to lead people out of their industrial and political trials? Fascists contend that such a system of electing re presentatives to direct the affairs of the nation is archaic.

It is no reply to argue that these elected representatives do not direct affairs. If they don't, why elect them? A new method must take the place of the old, and it must be a method that will not allow all the present evils of electioneering to take place. The electorate must be protected against a biased Press. It must have time to think coolly, to read sanely and to judge effectively. The electorate, too, must know the men whom they place in power.

Under the new system of government that Fascists will introduce, every section of the community will vote for those with whom it has a real identity of interest, for members of their own choice and from their own community, under a system of "occupational franchise."

A brief description of the agricultural corporation will indicate clearly what is meant by this "occupational franchise," as distinct from the present "geographical franchise." As every adult will vote, not according to his place of residence, but according to his occupation, it will mean that farmers will vote for farmers, nominated by themselves. Exactly the same will apply to agricultural labourers. Their candidates will be agricultural labourers, nominated by themselves and chosen by themselves. The elected farmers and elected labourers, with representatives of a Consumers' Council, and experts, such as agricultural research experts, accountants, etc., will be the Agricultural Corporation, and will have full authority over the production, distribution, and marketing of all agricultural commodities in Britain, including the control and sale of all agricultural products imported from the Dominions.

This will be real government of the farming community, by their own chosen representatives, living the same sort of life and experiencing the same sort of difficulties. This will be "government of the farming people, by the farming people, for the farming people," a truer conception of democracy than the present farce.

The election of representatives under such a system will for the first time give stability to government. Electors will not be swayed by appeals to "Hang the Kaiser," or scared by cries of the "Zinoviev letter." They will be deciding on issues of farming, of which they have real, practical knowledge.

This is the "occupational franchise" advocated by the British Union of Fascists, and to any unprejudiced mind, it will appeal as a reasonable change highly desirable for a new age.

ABOLITION OF THE PARLIAMENTARY SYSTEM

All this, of course, means the abolition of the present Parliamentary system. Why not? Parliament, as it is at Westminster, was created for a past age. It has not maintained its capacity to deal with problems that must be dealt with rapidly and energetically. Nobody, indeed, has a good word to say for the British House of Commons, or the House of Lords, with the possible exception of the official element of the Labour Party. Mr. Lansbury has so saturated himself with the spirit of the mother of Parliaments, that he is loathe to agree to any change. The official argument of Labour is that the Tories can work the machine of Parliament for their own purposes, and, therefore, so can Labour. They forget that the intention of the two parties is supposed to be entirely different. The Tory party, of course, can work the machine for their own ends for their desire is to do as little as possible, whereas the intention of the Labour Party, theoretically, at any rate, is to bring about a revolution in the whole economic system of the country.

The House of Commons is overwhelmed with arrears of work. There is no aspect of government with which it is abreast of the time. The Commons, realising its ignorance and inefficiency, delegated its authority to a Cabinet system that is the negation of leadership. The doctrine of Cabinet responsibility has intensified the negative character of government in this country. Ministers, after having been well tutored by their departments, have to discuss their detailed proposals with their fellow Cabinet Ministers who are uninformed men, harassed with the details of their own departments, and over-burdened with making week-end speeches and opening bazaars. Whatever decision is ultimately reached by the Cabinet is a compromise of the views of twelve, or more, ignorant men. The original decision is watered down, and lacks directness and clarity. On the altar of the doctrine of Cabinet Unity and responsibility, has been sacrificed many a sound scheme.

With elections conducted under sane, unemotional conditions, with the experts of the Corporation in control, the necessity for the double-barrelled method of government that has hitherto prevailed is removed. It is no doubt necessary in these days that there should be two Chambers at Westminster, each trying to prevent the other from making blunders, but under the new system of government this check will be unnecessary, and because it is unnecessary, the present archaic institution known as the House of Lords will disappear. In its place will be a group of experts and leaders of knowledge who will advise the Government on problems of the day. This Chamber will be nominated by the National Council of Industry.

WOMEN AND FASCISM

No system of government, however, would be complete, unless it made a substantial improvement in the political and economic status of women. It is true that women in this country have the vote, but it has not brought them economic liberty or economic salvation any more than the vote has brought those desirable assets to men.

Under the Fascist State, every woman engaged in industry, or in the profession, will possess a vote in the elections of her industrial or professional representatives. A woman lawyer, for instance, will possess a vote as a lawyer and will vote with all lawyers in selecting representatives to the central authority.

Further than this, women not engaged in "gainful" occupation, but who perform the important work of looking after the home and family, will elect their own repre sentatives, nominated and chosen by themselves. Women of the home will be represented by women of the home, and the nation will have the benefit of their experience in all matters appertaining to family life, health, education, dietary, housing and all the subjects in which women are so vitally interested.

LEADERSHIP OR DICTATORSHIP

Equally important in the Fascist philosophy of Government is that of Leadership, or Dictatorship as our opponents would prefer to say. If they mean by "Dictatorship," getting on with the job of governing when once the country has given a man the task of governing, then we are prepared to accept this description of

Dictatorship.

There is nothing more stupid than believing that in modern times, any one man, however powerful and strong willed, or however many machine-guns he may command, can govern a country against the will of the people. Government, inevitably today, is with the consent of the people, and a would-be tyrannical leader whose economic policy was not a success, would soon find that his own machine-gunners would use him as a target if there was no other way of getting rid of him.

Yet, the necessity of having a strong man at the helm, particularly when the country is passing through economic crisis, is obvious. Weak government must mean bad govern ment. Britain, in point of fact, has been crying out to its governments since the war, to get something done, but always the governments have been content to drift, or when they have been compelled to act, they have waited until it has been "too late." Always "too late!" Such an attitude nearly lost the war, and it has meant nothing but disaster ever since.

The Fascist attitude to government is quite simple. When a Fascist Government, with the consent of the people, is given the task of governing, it will get on with the job swiftly and efficiently, and, knowing that it possesses the confidence of the majority of the people, and is acting on behalf of the majority, will not tolerate opposition from any minority or sectional interests. The minority has rights, but it has not the right to hold up schemes that are desired by the majority of the people of the country. Fascists will govern, and selfish interests will be subordinated to the common will, no matter how powerful those interests have been in the past.

3 - Organising the Food Front

The very basis of Blackshirt policy is the imperative and absolute necessity of building up a home market to replace the loss of the greater part of the overseas market, which, it is generally agreed, is inevitable. This can be achieved only by a vigorous and prosperous countryside.

In agriculture will be found an important part of the solution to the problem of Britain's economic future. Blackshirts insist on the restoration of prosperity to the agricultural community for four reasons:

First: the economic future of the nation demands that lost foreign markets should be replaced by permanent home markets.

Second: the agricultural industry is most suitable for rapid and extensive expansion and can absorb not only the unemployed farm workers and farm tenants, but can find employment for vast numbers of unemployed from the industrial areas, who after suitable training under experts, would be taken into the agricultural industry.

Third: a system of owner-occupier farms will give to many thousands of our people a sense of possessing a real stake in the country.

Fourth: cultivation of the soil imparts both to the individual and the community an indefinable spiritual value that is associated with the expression "Yeomen of Old England."

Britain blundered during the last century when she allowed her agricultural industry to fall into decay, and "Back to the Land" has been raised frequently as a political cry. This political cry has not yet had any results and in no other country today is there such a small proportion of the people living on the land. In France, over forty per cent, of the population draw their sustenance from the soil; in Germany over thirty per cent; in Belgium nearly twenty per cent, whereas in Britain the number is less than ten per cent. Although since 1913 Britain's population has increased by about five per cent, she is now importing about thirty per cent more food than she did before the war. From the point of view of economic independence, therefore, Britain's position today is worse than it was in 1914.

Britain must use all her skill, all her man-power, and all her financial resources to develop her agricultural industry. She must make the fullest use of the land resources that she has available, and she must increase those resources by a vigorous policy of "Home Colonisation," based on reclamation schemes.

One of the first tasks that a Fascist Government in Britain will put in hand is the colonisation of the country. The people of this country have played their part in colonising the world. Now they must have the opportunity of colonising Britain.

The facts regarding post-war emigration are not sufficiently realised. Whereas before the war we used to send thousands of our best men to the far quarters of the world, in the last couple of years emigration has not only ceased, but, as a matter of fact, the number of returned emigrants to Britain has exceeded those who have left its shores. In view of the reluctance of the overseas Empire to absorb more citizens of these islands in the immediate present, the alternative is to colonise Britain.

It is useless declaring that the country is over-populated when there is far less land under cultivation now than there was some years ago; and when the land actually under cultivation is not being used to its utmost extent.

There are many farmers in this country, indeed, one might go so far as to say most farmers, who could easily double their output if a constructive farming policy was inaugurated by a Government. Farmers would respond magnificently to any move that would enable them to increase the pro ductivity of their land.

Britain has hundreds of thousands of acres available that she could use, if she would only take up a scheme of land reclamation.

Some years ago The Times declared: "Hundreds of thousands of acres of what might be valuable and productive land, both above and below high-tide mark, are left derelict for want of the labour and energy necessary to reclaim them from the dominion of the river and seas and to bring them under cultivation."

The position since those lines were penned is unchanged. Britain has vast stretches of land that she could reclaim and convert into first-class agricultural land. There is no technical reason why the Wash should not be rescued from the seas. Other countries have carried through gigantic schemes of this character and they have been able to add considerably to the amount of land available for agriculture.

While other countries have acted on the lines now suggested, Britain has been content with her leisurely policy of appointing Royal Commissions. Such a Commission in 1927 declared that over a million acres suffered from flooding caused by defective or obstructed arterial channels. The Commission called attention to the serious need for land drainage, and to the real possibility that in the course of time, more and more land would become water-logged, thereby, of course, destroying its utility value to the community. Since then, as might be expected, nothing has been done, and nothing is likely to be done until a Fascist Government is charged with governing the country.

Other countries, however, are not asleep, and one can find sufficient proof of the practicability of land reclamation by examining the activities of other countries.

In Fascist Italy, a vigorous scheme of what they style "home colonising" has been taking place for several years, and is being continued. Under a special division of the Italian Ministry of Agriculture, systematic schemes of land reclamation and irrigation are being carried out, coupled with the construction of roads, aqueducts, schools and other public buildings, farm workers' dwellings, etc. Hundreds of families from the crowded areas of the country have been permanently settled in these new provinces.

The comment on these schemes of the British Counsellor to the British Embassy at Rome is: "results have been obtained which are of positive and of permanent value." Italy's example, however, is not isolated, and if Britain is still waiting patiently for some other country to give her concrete examples of what can be done, she might well turn her attention to other European countries.

The reclamation of the Zuyder Zee, of course, is a well-known example, and what Holland can do there, in converting a watery waste into a fertile country, Britain might well do with the Wash. But the Zuyder Zee is not the only activity of the Dutch in land reclamation, and altogether that country now enjoys the products of a quarter of a million acres that at one time were either under water permanently or so seriously subject to floods that they were useless.

Bringing into use these vast territories, however, will be entirely useless from the point of view of agricultural prosperity unless such activity is accompanied by definite moves to improve farming, and to ensure that farmers received a fair price for their products.

In the past, this country has concentrated on a policy of obtaining cheap food for her people for the sole reason that manufacturers in our cities desired to keep down the cost of living, thereby enabling them to pay low wages, so that they could sell cheap products in foreign lands.

This insistence on low wages and cheap food meant that Britain had to import the greater part of her foodstuffs. Today the position has changed. No device of British manufacturers, not even if they forced wages down 50 per cent of their present level, would enable them to regain their markets, and Britain, therefore, under the changed circumstances must change her tactics, and concentrate on bringing prosperity to her countryside.

The employment of people in healthy, gainful occupation on the land will put an end to a system which compels men and women to live in over-crowded, dirty cities, queuing up at Labour Exchanges to draw miserable pittances that are insufficient to enable human beings to live on a level worthy of the twentieth century. Such a result will be of immense advantage to the physical and mental development of our people, enabling hundreds of thousands of people to enjoy higher real wages, better homes, clothing, and a greater share of the luxuries of the world.

This increased demand would in its turn bring prosperity to our great industrial centres, which will welcome the prospect of improved sales to people enjoying a higher standard of living. It will be argued that 2,000,000 odd agricultural workers in this country is an inadequate substitute for the lost markets of Africa and Asia. So it is, but this two million is a nucleus of a guaranteed market, which will help to find work for the towns and cities of our land until such time as the Empire develops a more orderly interchange of commodities.

Before describing in detail the Fascist Policy for the revival of agriculture, it is well worth while examining the causes of the failures of the schemes recently put forward by the Conservative Party. The failure of these schemes is due primarily because the Government has not exercised vigorous control over imports, and has failed to bring about any increase in the consuming power of the people. Mr. Elliot recently told the country that there were approximately one million workers on the land, feeding about 20,000,000 of our population, and he warned the country of potential difficulties in the matter of overseas trade if a further million were settled on the land to feed the other 20,000,000.

Mr. Elliot is disturbed lest any scheme for placing more men on the land should result in the loss of the export trade. He overlooks the cardinal fact that a substantial part of the export trade has gone and will continue to go, irrespective of whether we place another million men on the land or not. As our export trade diminishes in the future, we will not be able to buy food from abroad. That is, we will have to become accustomed to a lower standard of living. Many of our people will be too impoverished to buy food. The alternative before Britain is: We must either produce our own food or starve.

It is said, with some show of statistical authority that this country in modern times, cannot feed her present population. Even if it were true that Britain cannot feed herself for fifty-two weeks of the year, that is no reason why she should not attempt to feed herself for forty or fifty weeks, and on a much higher standard of living than that which prevails today.

Another factor, and indeed probably the main factor, that has influenced Mr. Elliot's plans is that the Conservative Party is highly involved in international finance. To attempt to interfere with foreign imports, and particularly with the beef imports from the Argentine, would greatly jeopardise the interest on the loans that the City of London has made to the Argentine in the past.

The reluctance to regard these loans and the "interest" as "bad debts" can well be understood, but when a choice has to be made, as a choice has to be made now, between past financial transactions with foreign borrowers, or the whole future of British agriculture and British economic stability, then Britain's future interests must prevail.

The Conservative Party, however, is afraid of offending the financial interests of London and, therefore, declines to interfere with imports of foreign meat, greatly to the detriment of the British live-stock industry. Mr. Elliot's political ideology therefore, prevents his embarking on a more vigorous scheme of increasing agricultural production. If he produces more he thinks it will mean less imports and in the long run will injure our export trade. Encompassed in a mental prison of this character he is unable to go forward with any real scheme.

Mr. Elliot's schemes have failed for the further important reason that he has done nothing to raise the consuming power of the public. Until the general public has the power to buy more commodities from the farmers, then no agricultural policy can possibly be successful. A rapid increase in the standard of living is essential for the sake of the people themselves, and for the sake of the farming community as well.

It is agreed that the vast majority of our people are under fed. Most men and women in work could eat better food even if they did not eat greater quantities. Anybody who has lived among the working classes knows that they are compelled through economic circumstances over which neither they nor the tradesmen have any control, to eat substantial quantities of food that contain practically no nourishment whatever. Many have to eat coarse bread without butter, cheap bacon, foreign meat of low quality - thousands have to be content with "fish and chips" as the main meal of the day. The food they eat is poor in quality, lacks nourishment and is unpalatable. There is no real reason for supposing that the standard of living, so far as food is concerned, could not be raised by at least twenty per cent - probably far more - and even then it could not be said that the masses of the people were over fed and over-nourished. British fresh meats, vegetables, milk and fruits are unexcelled in quality and command a preference on the British market. They should be available to the whole of our people and not only to a minority.

Fascism would deal with the whole subject of foreign foodstuffs with characteristic energy. These goods would be completely prohibited and the British people would enjoy first-class British food, which, by the Fascist policy of increasing wages, they would be able to purchase. Then, with an assured market of 45,000,000 people, the farmers would produce practically all the foodstuffs required, obtaining certain categories, which cannot be grown here, from the Dominions. This would mean more work for a larger farming community, all of whom would be spending their money here in Britain on British manufactured goods.

The Agricultural Corporation would ensure a fair division of the increased prosperity between the farmers and the workers, and having complete control over production and distribution would be able to give the public a first-class service, at a reasonable cost.

4 - Imports, Exports and Shipping

While a strong, vigorous policy for the restoration of prosperity to agriculture is the essence of Fascist policy, Blackshirts realise that this is not sufficient. The manufacturing centres of Britain, too, must be assisted by measures of definite value.

Revival of agriculture will, indirectly, assist the great industrial areas by providing them with an increased demand to take the place of a reduced demand from overseas, but it will still be necessary to give them direct assistance.

Fascists face up to this reality and declare emphatically that the only possible way in which it can be done is to prohibit completely, the importation of all those categories of manufactured goods that can be made here.

The amount of goods that will come under this classification may vary from time to time, but that it is considerable in volume and value, cannot be gainsaid. An imposing array of statistics over which so-called experts might quarrel is unnecessary here. The imported foreign goods can be seen by everybody who cares to glance in the shop windows of our thoroughfares. They range over almost every class of industry, but particularly do they affect textiles and fancy goods. Foreign competition is severe in the lighter engineering trades, and in also what are called the "newer" industries.

Foreign goods can, and must be kept out, and a Fascist Government will not hesitate to put an embargo on them. The old methods of tariffs and quotas have proved to be absolutely insufficient to protect the British manufacturer from foreign competition. Foreign competitors have the direct and indirect aid of the governmental devices of subsidies and deliberate currency depreciations and bounties, by which they can overcome all the attempts to reduce imports by means of the tariff weapon. In the interests of British industries it is imperative that imports should be kept down to the lowest possible level and that the only imports from overseas should be those categories of goods which cannot be produced, either in Britain or in the Empire.

Overseas Trade

Britain will always be compelled to import commodities which for climatic reasons she cannot produce herself. She will always have to import from the overseas Empire some kinds of foodstuffs, such as certain grades of wheat, cotton, and some classes of wool, hard woods, and other commodities that obviously she cannot produce at home.

To pay for these imports it will be necessary to retain as much of her export trade as she possibly can and she can only do this by entering into definite trading agreements with Empire buyers and sellers. The longer that this task is left undone, the greater will be the difficulty of entering into such agreements, and when ultimately it has to be done, the greater the danger to Britain's economic future.

Fascists emphasise that such trading agreements can be best achieved among the nations that comprise the British Commonwealth. As time goes on the difficulty of developing inter-Empire trade must increase. The great Dominions like Canada and Australia have quite naturally endeavoured to build up their own secondary industries and it would be too much to expect them to lose the capital that they have invested in these industries and to throw out of employment the workers who now find their livelihood in them. It is one of the criminal follies of Empire post-war statesmen that they have allowed such a situation to develop. Every day's delay makes the situation increasingly difficult. A quick return of Fascists to power in Britain would arrest the conflict of interests that is growing up between the nations within the Empire.

Permanent Imperial Economic Council

We will make it our first duty both in the interests of Britain and of the Dominions and Colonies, to bring into session a permanent Imperial Economic Council which will concentrate the whole of its attention on this one problem of exchanging goods between the constituent parts of the Empire. New and improved trading agreements which would include the exchange of raw materials for manufacturing goods will be drawn up. The fact that this Council will be in constant session will be a great advance on the system of spasmodic meetings of statesmen at occasional Imperial Conferences, at which energy is more often than not directed at adjusting constitutional, legal and other problems.

SHIPPING AND SHIPBUILDING

The problem of shipping and shipbuilding cannot be faced with any understanding, unless it is appreciated that the old pre-war export trade can never be regained. Realisation of this fact, however, is not a policy of despair: it is a policy of realism, and the greatest enemy that these to related industries possess is that blind optimist who talks glibly about the glories of international trade under the impression that at some future time Britain will once more enjoy practically a monopoly of the world's carrying.

Other nations have learned how to build ships, and, where they have not, they have learned the secret of buying up old British ships to navigate them on seas where the British flag, once predominant, now rarely flies. Especially is this true of some of the Near Eastern routes, where Greek shipping companies, having bought British ships practically at scrap prices—from British banks in most cases—are operating them with cheap labour.

Other mercantile navies are being built up, and British ships no longer carry the bulk of the world's goods. This fact, reinforced by the rise of "economic nationalism," a phenomena that was inevitable, makes the pre-war prosperity of British shipping a part of history.

Some rehabilitation, however, is possible, if the interests of Britain are put first, and Sir Oswald Mosley has laid down a Five-Point Policy for shipping which will advance the interests of British shipping, and eventually of British shipbuilding.

These Five Points are:

1. British coastal trade to be kept for British ships.
2. Empire trade to be kept for British ships.
3. Only British crews for British ships.
4. White crews in all British ships outside the tropics.
5. No more sales of old British ships to foreign shipping firms, to be used by them to undercut British freights.

As a further measure, to rid the country of the glut of shipping that will never be used again, and also, to provide the shipyards with work, Fascists propose, when they are in power, to scrap all ships over 20 years old and to modernise the mercantile marine with new ships.

Such a measure, we realise, is inadequate to provide shipyards of the Clyde, North East and Belfast with work up to their capacity, but that is not the fault of Fascists. It is the direct consequence of the orgy of building that succeeded the shortage caused by the war. The irresponsible attitude of ship-owners who ordered vessels, for which there has never been anything like adequate work, is a legacy of the old system. And you cannot expect people who have created chaos in any industry, to remove that chaos. Their mismanagement has had terrible economic results, and only a new approach to the problem can possibly put the shipbuilding industry on its feet again.

5 - The Power of Finance

No economic or industrial reconstruction is possible without rigid control of finance. There are, moreover, strong political reasons for such control.

Financiers have acquired so much power that they have become the greatest power in the land, greater than Parliament, or any other institution.

This is not essentially a Fascist view. It is one that will be endorsed by Mr. Ramsay Muir, the arch-priest of the gospel of non-interference by Governments. In his book, "How Britain is Governed," Mr. Ramsay Muir has summarised and described the power of finance most concisely. "The control of finance," says Mr. Muir, "even more than the control of legislation, is supposed to be the peculiar prerogative of Parliament. The influence over the financial policy of the Government that is wielded by Parliament - more particularly when the Government has got a majority - is negligible in comparison with the influence that is wielded by the power that is conveniently summarised as "the City" - the power of the Banks, the big financial houses and the Stock Exchange. This influence is exercised, not at all through Parliament, but by direct and private pressure upon the Chancellor of the Exchequer and the Treasury, and this pressure is all but irresistible because of the frequent operations of the Treasury in the money-market."

In a sentence, the position of the Government is that of a borrower. The City exercises the "pressure," as Mr. Muir calls it, that a money-lender exercises over a frequent borrower of money. This alone is sufficient reason for the demand of Fascists for greater control over "the City," but it is reinforced by the inability of the City itself to control its own speculators and wasters who dissipate, without a blush, the fortunes of the trusting investing public.

Some illuminating information was given by the then President of the Society of Incorporated Accountants, at the end of September, 1930, which revealed the callous indifference of the City to the welfare of investors. During the last six months of 1928, there were advertised in a particular newspaper the prospectuses of fifty-eight companies. The President had examined the fate of those fifty-eight companies and had found, two years after they had been advertised, that only one had paid a dividend. Twenty-seven were already in liquidation and at least sixteen others were in serious difficulties. Of the total capital, no less than ninety-five per cent, had been lost.

These losses were in the ordinary course of business and must not be confused with the gigantic losses lost in the over-capitalisation of the Lancashire cotton mills, the fortunes lost in the Kreuger, Bottomley and Hatry swindles, or the tremendous "writing down" of capital of all the big companies. With ordinary prudence and control practically the whole of these losses could have been avoided.

Judged by the standpoint of efficiency alone, "the City" is condemned as a danger to the financial resources of the country.

The Gold Standard

All these occurrences, however, pale into insignificance when compared with the huge theft perpetrated on industry by the financiers who persuaded the British post-war Governments to embark on the policy known as the "return to the Gold Standard."

Perhaps if the war had never occurred, the gold standard would have held undisputed sway for many generations to come, but the war created inter-Governmental debts, and internal debts, that demanded, if they were to have the ghost of a chance of being paid, that the pound should maintain its war-time level.

Many of the inter-Governmental debts, of course, have been

repudiated, either wholly or partially, by one device or another, and where they have not been, the creditors concerned have agreed to accept amounts much less than they advanced. Some countries, too, have "disposed" of their internal debts by devices such as depreciation of the currency, but Britain chose to play a "heroic" part: she rose to the occasion, and increased the burden of internal debt by manipulating the currency.

In terms of goods and services—and goods and services are the kernel of the last analysis—Britain increased her internal debt by something like a third. It is easy to under stand what happened if one regards goods in terms of units. The pound note at the end of the war could be exchanged for approximately 13 units. By 1925 the bankers carried out their operations to such an extent that the pound note could be exchanged for 20 units.

The middle-classes and workers, in the intervening years, had suffered wage and salary reductions to a corresponding extent and as they were receiving fewer notes, their income, in terms of goods, was lower. But one class of the community, and this was mainly the banking community, found that its stream of notes was steadily maintained, and they were getting more and more units of goods which industry was having to provide.

It is true that since 1931, Mr. Neville Chamberlain has carried out certain "conversion" schemes, which have reduced the figure 20 to about 18, but even so, the rentier class is receiving more than was implied in the contract, and it is doing this when many other people, particularly those who are engaged in industry, whether employers or employed, are having to accept less.

Apart from the question of the morality of giving this class of person more than was implied in the contract, it proved, in the end to be economically unsound. Industry had to provide those extra items of goods, and there came a point, in 1931, when industry was unable to bear the burden any longer.

This appropriation of extra produce from industry, of course, was not done altogether blindly. The politicians who carried out the policy knew that they would be increasing the income of all who held Government bonds. It was, as a matter of fact, the greatest theft that has ever been carried out in broad daylight. The politicians knew what was happening and every step that was taken was with their concurrence.

The method by which the return to the gold standard was operated was comparatively simple. Money and credit was plentiful at the 1919 and 1920 period. There was a scarcity of goods and everybody was called upon "to produce more" and to work harder. Banks were lending freely and credit could be had for the mere asking, and when money and credit increase, so do prices. In fact, things were going the wrong way. The pound note was bringing in less than they wanted—so the machine must be reversed, the pound note must bring in more. This could only be done by decreasing prices. Bringing prices down is just as easy as increasing them.

To increase prices, bankers issue more money and credit; to decrease prices they reduce money and credit. So the financiers and bankers in 1921 started their game. The pound must be a real golden pound. Credit, therefore, was called in right and left. Business after business was closed down. Thousands, hundreds of thousands of working people, were thrown out of the mills, pits, workshops and offices to queue up at the Labour Exchanges. Prices and wages came tumbling down. Until 1931, world conditions became steadily worse and collapse was unavoidable.

Almost everywhere since then "gold" has been thrown over. Even in the United States there has been wholesale repudiation of obligations to pay in terms of gold because of the intolerable burden resting on farmers. The "gold clause" has been eliminated from contracts and now, only bankers have a good word to say for gold.

The control of finance, therefore, is important in the economic life of the nation, for in the end it is one of the main factors in determining the standard of living of the people and the rate of progress of industrial expansion.

MANAGED CURRENCY

Fascists will not hesitate to exercise that control through a special Financial Corporation that will be set up, charged with the responsibility of controlling investments at home and abroad - in view of the immense wealth lost and the international complications resulting, overseas investments must be regarded with extreme disfavour - directing capital and credit into those channels most essential from an industrial point of view.

Currency management must be fundamental to any modern society, for it is the only method by which the balance of production and consumption can possibly be maintained. We have already seen that at a time when the process of production was being rapidly and extensively speeded up, when the capacity for producing more goods of all sorts was being increased almost a hundredfold, for reasons already given, this country allowed itself to be persuaded into a policy of contracting money and credit. Expansion of production on one hand, and contraction of consumption on the other, was the policy that the country was trying to operate.

It may seem like stating the obvious when one declares that as the capacity for production increases, so should the capacity for consumption (that is, money and credit which allows the commodities to be consumed). This simple, matter of fact statement, will hardly be contradicted. It must be apparent that production and consumption should run on parallel lines and should not diverge. If consumption is contracted, and production expanded, then only one thing can happen; that is, goods that are made will not be purchased, production will slow down, people will be thrown out of work and prices will fall. That is exactly what did happen. The lines, instead of being compelled to run parallel, were compelled to diverge, and industry ran badly off the lines.

Fascists declare emphatically that this need not have happened, and under their control, will not happen. Production and consumption can be balanced and must be balanced to such a degree of accuracy that there will be little waste caused by producing things that are not required by society, and also that no essential commodity will be too dear for the masses of the people. This involves managed production and managed consumption, that is, a "managed currency."

Few are left who will deny that a managed currency is desirable, and none are left who will contend that currency cannot be managed. The fact is, of course, that currency is being continuously "managed," and has been managed either by financiers and politicians since the end of the war. Particularly has the official management been in operation since the establishment of the Exchange Equalisation Fund by Mr. Neville Chamberlain. With this fund of £350,000,000, Mr. Chamberlain has been engaged in "managing" the value of sterling in relation to the American dollar and the French franc. The external value of sterling has been kept where Mr. Chamberlain has desired it to be.

Managing the external value of currency, however, has produced a currency war between nations, which has yet to be fought out and, therefore, it is imperative that even in matters of currency, some attempt at insulation should be made. One helpful factor from the British point of view is that other countries, both in and out of the Empire, take sterling as their standard, and there exists quite an important "sterling group" of countries.

Internally, however, there is no reason why the pound should not be kept in a definite relationship to goods. This does not imply that always, in terms of commodities, the pound should always purchase the exact amount of any given commodity today, as it did yesterday, or as it will tomorrow, but rather that the amount of commodities that a pound will command, should not be left to chance, or to the whim of some minor section of the community such as a group of producers, distributors or financiers, but that its value should be determined with some definite object in view.

For instance, if it were considered necessary, from the point of view of the State, and not from the point of view of the farmer, or miller, or anybody else, that the production of wheat in this country should be curtailed, the fixation of the price of wheat could be at such a low figure that its production would automatically decrease. Alternatively, if it were desired to produce more wheat, the method of offering a higher price would have the necessary results.

One result would be that the producers would be assured of a known price before embarking on production. It would mean that for the first time, undesirable gambling and speculation would be divorced from production. No scheme of industrial organisation or agricultural activity can attain satisfactory results if the producers are working in the dark without any knowledge of marketing prices. Stability under such an organisation would give industry a chance to function without the continuous fear that the goods would be sold at a loss, or would be left unsold.

Thus would finance be restored to its historic role, the servant of industry, not its master. Equally important would be the political results, for it would mean that once more the government would govern the country, free from the "pressure" of which Mr. Muir wrote. Britain then would be released from bondage.

6 - Religion and Race

The determination on the part of the British Union of Fascists to remove the burden of tithes from agriculture does not indicate any antagonism towards the Church of England. On the contrary, we believe that it is in the best interests of both the established Church and of the agricultural community that the friction which has been engendered by the tithe system should be ended for reasons which I have already given.

It is well, however, that Fascists should define their whole attitude towards religion and the denominations into which it is divided. We stand absolutely and completely for a policy of non-interference in religious controversy and activity, and will, so far as we are able, take all possible steps to encourage and assist all sections of religious thought to revive the religious fervour of the country. The leaders of religion will remain leaders and there will be no interference with them, and it will be the duty of the State to give what assistance they can in stimulating religious activity.

This they can do best by increasing the facilities for religious education. Denominational schools are an important branch of religious teaching, and religious organisations that modernise their schools will be assisted financially to do so in the joint interests of religion and education. Such aid will be given without discrimination between denominations. The provision of such facilities, of course, will not mean that religious education will be compulsory. The non-religious community have, and must have, as much freedom of choice in these matters, as the religious.

THE RACIAL PROBLEM

The racial problem in Britain is not so intensified as it is in some other parts of the world, but there does exist, even in this country, the necessity of protecting our shores from invasion by non-desirable types. This principle is one that has been accepted by this and other countries in the past, and most countries have had to pass legislation to protect themselves from peoples of other countries. The United States, Australia, New Zealand and South Africa have been compelled to pass such protective laws.

Britain, too, in the past has had to deal with this problem of foreigners desiring to make their homes here. There was an "invasion" of this country by Jews from Prussia, Poland and the South European countries in the closing years of last century with the result that in 1902 a Royal Commission was appointed to report on the subject of foreign pauper immigration. The Aliens Act was passed in 1905, making it compulsory for a would-be immigrant to show that he was able to support himself and his dependents, and that he was physically and mentally sound. The principle of a nation defending itself, therefore, from an inflow of undesirable peoples is not new, but under the new Fascist system of Government, it would be made harder, if not impossible, for foreign peoples to settle here on an island that has already a population far greater, in proportion to size, than most other countries. "Britain for British people" is an ideal, surely, that must commend itself generally. It is not as though we were a new country thinly populated and anxious to open up new territories. The actual position is just the reverse.

With work so scarce here, there is no justification for allowing foreign nationals to come to this country and compete in the labour market and accept a lower rate of wages than that which British workmen would tolerate. "British workmen for British work" is not asking too much.

So far as foreign people already living here are concerned, so long as they conform to British standards, as laid down by the Fascist State, they will be permitted to live and work on exactly the same basis as British subjects. There will be no discrimination and no persecution because of race or religion.

Foreigners, however, who break the economic code of

Fascism, or the social code, will be deported. This happens already in criminal affairs. A foreigner who is a habitual criminal or a social pest, is deported by the Home Office, because this country, quite rightly, has no use for residents of this character.

The criminal in industry, however, is ignored and allowed to operate. A foreigner, who, for his own selfish gain, adopts in industry a hard, cruel policy of overworking boys and girls and pays them niggardly wages, who attacks every standard of remuneration that has been won by years of trade union organisation, is definitely a criminal in industry, doing intense harm, and is, in every way, undesirable. Under Fascist Government in Britain, he will be deported without hesitation.

All that we shall insist upon is that all people in this country shall observe a code of conduct in their social and economic relations. British citizens who do not observe them will be dealt with by the British courts, as at present constituted; but foreigners, whether they are big financiers, operating from the City of London, or grasping little trades men of Whitechapel, will be deported.

If, however, they observe the economic and social laws of the country and observe the Fascist rule of "Britain First" they will have nothing to fear. The reign of the unscrupulous foreigner must come to an end in this country.

7 - The Price of Liberty

"The price of liberty is eternal vigilance." This is a truer saying than many who quote it realise. Encroachments are continually being made on the liberty of the individual and very often the individual lacks appreciation of the net that is closing in on him. He is indifferent, and goes along in sublime ignorance of the significance of events.

The chief criticism of Fascism, based on the allegation

that it is an infringement of the liberty of the people, and that it intends to set up a harsh, cruel dictatorship, comes curiously enough from the Communists. They pose as the champions of the working-classes, and hold up Fascists as oppressors and reactionaries. "The Fascist will take your liberty from you," say the Communists, "they will expose you to terrorism, cast you into concentration camps," and then, the Communists, in their next peroration, will tell the working-classes that they are but "wage-slaves," with nothing to lose but their chains. To take "liberty" from slaves is a task that not even Fascists can perform.

But the Communists know better. They have read the case for Fascism in Britain and they understand our case perfectly. They know that it would bring wealth and prosperity to our country, but because of their worship of a political philosophy, they prostitute every decent feeling and impulse within them, to invent violent, vicious lies about Fascism and Fascist policy.

Why should the Communists complain that Fascists want to set up a dictatorship? They do not oppose the principle of dictatorship. Indeed, its acceptance is part of their fundamental political system. Communists jibe at capitalists who, they allege control the Press and the schools. Are we to assume that there is no control of the Press in Russia and no control of the schools? Are Russian teachers at liberty to teach whatever they like, and the Press to print whatever they please? Of course not. The Communists believe in a controlled Press, controlled propaganda, and a dictatorship. All that they object to is the control being exercised by the other fellow. They want to be dictators themselves.

There is, however, a greater, and a far more important volume of criticism that comes from the democratic parties of Conservatism, Liberalism and Socialism. They are convinced, so it would seem from the utterances of their leaders, that Fascism would mean a definite curtailment in the liberty of the individual and that it would result in the creator of a dictatorship.

It is well that this charge of dictatorship should be closely examined, for people in this land, and they are wise in this, hold tenaciously to the ideal of liberty—religious liberty and civil liberty—and are entitled to it. Absolute liberty, however, is unattainable. If it were attempted, nothing but anarchy would result. In practice, the curtailment of liberty is accepted by all, and it is generally agreed that every man should be allowed to do as he pleases, so long as he does no harm to anyone else. Such a statement is a common place in politics. Indeed, society goes further and will not allow a man to do as he likes, even if he is not harming anybody but is harming himself. It is held, for instance, to be an offence against society, to attempt to put an end to one's life, even if the would-be suicide can have no injurious effect upon anybody excepting himself.

Society is eminently sensible on this question of regulation of liberty. It calls upon the individual to sacrifice many rights and keeps on multiplying the demands on the ground that the surrender of the individual right is essential if the welfare of Society is to be considered. All social legislation is based on this. In nearly all trades, for instance, a workman is not permitted to work unless he is prepared to agree to a deduction from his remuneration for health and unemployment insurances. His employer has not the "right" to make him work on dangerous machinery unless the machinery is protected. There is no "right" or "liberty" in a thousand and one ways in industry. Certain industries are not permitted, under the system of Trade Boards, to pay their work-people below a certain fixed rate.

All these, and many, many others, are infringements on the liberty of the individual, which were not in existence so very many years ago. So we find that liberty is curtailed to a great extent already. Yet every great advance in social organisation has been bitterly opposed by these champions of liberty.

All social organisation must necessarily involve a curtail ment on the liberty and activities of the individual, but the price is worth paying if it results in better health and comfort for a majority of the people. Every great advance in the liberty of mankind has been opposed by the allegation that the suggested advance is an attack on liberty. In our own time the great schemes of Health Insurance, Unemployment Insurance, the abolition of half-time labour in the textiles mills of the North and other measures designed to improve the social and economic position of the working classes have been similarly opposed by this cry of "liberty."

So it is with Fascism. The reactionaries who want to continue to exploit any section of the community in their own selfish interests, the financiers who want to gull the public out of their money; the international moneylenders and "rings" and "trusts" in industry, all these are combined with the "liberty-mongers" to make a united front against the next step in the liberation of the people against poverty.

The masses of the people need not fear Fascism in Britain. They will work as they work now, but they will live and work under better conditions; they will have better homes, better facilities for enjoyment, for keeping themselves fit, for playing the games they love so well, for music, literature, for greater and better libraries, for everything that makes life worth living. The benefits of the advances in science and industry will be their servants. New and better machinery, instead of throwing the people into poverty, will provide them with a greater share of the riches of the world. The middle-classes, too, will notice no change in their lives excepting changes for the better.

The only sections of the community who will find that a Fascist State will put a curb on their activities will be those who organise themselves for the purposes of furthering their own advantages at the expense of the community. The Fascist Government will not allow itself to be dictated to by any clique of financiers, bankers, or trade union leaders who desire to serve their own interests. Nor will representatives of sectional interests be permitted to agitate against the Fascist Government with the object of over throwing it or frustrating its efforts to carry out its schemes. This does not mean that aggrieved sections of the community will not have full opportunity to state their point of view. They will be given a fair hearing, and if there is substance in their case, their wishes will prevail. But attempts to ruin the schemes designed at producing better conditions for the whole of the people will not be tolerated.

The benefit of the whole, and not of any section, will be the guiding rule of Fascists when they are in power. This is not tyranny; it is a fair and just view based on common sense.

Fascism will give the individual the maximum liberty that can be obtained from the highly complex social organisation that is inevitable; he will find greater scope for the develop ment of his intellectual and physical faculties; his only obligations will be to take his part in the production of the wealth that he will himself enjoy and to play his part as a citizen of a truly great nation. His duties will be no heavier than they are at present while the opportunity to live a life freer from economic stress will be greater.

8 - Fascism, Trade Unions and the Workers

Fascists acknowledge that their new creed has been inspired by the century-old struggle of the workers towards unity. Instead of being antagonistic towards the workers, as opponents allege, Fascism is the logical outcome of the Trade Union movement's fight for fair conditions.

The working-classes of Britain can truthfully claim that they have paved the way for the modern movement of Fascism. When they were completely at the mercy of unscrupulous employers at the beginning of the industrial revolution, they created their Trade Unions as a measure of protection; they built up the gigantic organisations of Friendly Societies to form the pattern for National Health Insurance; and their third organisation, that of the Co-operative Societies preceded the large chain stores that have sprung up everywhere today.

This three-fold struggle of a hundred years and more has been directed against cut-throat competition, against individualism and against exploitation by profit-mongers.

The workers were at least generations ahead of the so-called captains of industry and the smug intellectuals who have stood outside the ring watching the struggle between capitalists and workers. When mechanical industry was still young, workers knew that unity was the source of strength. They despised the blackleg as an immoral enemy of his class, as one who, fighting under the shoddy banner of freedom, maintained that he had the right to work at lower wages than the standard rate, and under whatever conditions he liked, irrespective of the harm it did to his fellow-workmen.

The workers fought the "blackleg" in and out of industry generations. Sometimes they were successful and sometimes they lost, but always the workers retained the undying spirit to fight on.

Half-heartedly the employers and financiers learned the lessons that the workmen had taught them. They formed themselves into federations and cartels and created their price-rings, but even today, industry is still in a state of anarchy. For the vastly shrunken trade of the world there are still thousands of manufacturers and merchants engaged in a bitter struggle, one against the other, cutting prices wherever they can, bringing ruin upon themselves and endeavouring to beat down the working-classes to a lower standard of living in order to secure a share of diminishing trade. This is true of almost every industry and particularly of wool and cotton textiles, iron and steel, and also of the coal export trade, as well as many others.

The Next Stage in Evolution

Fascism is the next stage in the evolution of industrial structure. The two cardinal principles of unity and co-operation, which the workers have exercised for so long, must permeate through the whole of industry to the national life. They mean the death of individualism and anarchy, the death of chaos and disorder, and the final triumph over the individual who claims the right to do as he pleases. Therefore, Fascism appeals with confidence to earnest trade unionists. The new system is but an advance on everything that they have fought for in the past, and Fascism demands "a union for every worker and every worker in his union."

The workers today are justified in their demand for a substantial advance in their standard of living. Above all, they contend that the grave uncertainty and the mental anguish caused by unemployment should be removed.

They are anxious to participate in the creation of a new world in which all men and women and children will be assured of a reasonable standard of comfort, an adequate supply of food, a home which will be a real home in every sense of the word, in which no person will go ill-clad, and in which they will be able to enjoy some of the luxuries that the middle-classes and rich people now take for granted. The workers complain—and they are justified in complaining—that they are not allowed to help in creating such a new world, but rather are they regarded as pieces of machinery to be brought into use when someone can employ them for profit-making purposes, after which they can be thrown on to the scrap-heap. The workers are justified in demanding an advance in their material welfare comparable to the greater advance that has taken place in education and culture, in invention and science.

To attain this they realise that extensive re-organisation in industry will be required if their just demands are to be met, and they ask as one of the main constituent parts of industry, having a real contribution to make, they should be allowed to do their part. They claim that re-organisation must precede prosperity and that industry must have unity of purpose.

These are legitimate demands of the workers, which through the machinery of the Corporate State will be satisfied. The Corporate State stands for exactly the same principles as those on which the trade union movement were founded, unity and collective action.

This Corporate State will be well equipped for dealing with the many problems that affect the industrial labour market, such as foreign competition, rationalisation, the decay of old industries, and rise of new ones, and such problems as the transfer of labour. Such an organisation will be required to an even greater degree in the future.

Since the war there has been a gradual shrinkage in the number of workers in such industries as mining, agriculture, textiles, engineering, iron and steel, shipbuilding, and more workers have been taken into the distributive and luxury trades, such as electrical apparatus, motor vehicles, artificial silk, transport, banking, insurance, sports, entertainments, local government and so on.

Such a tendency was inevitable and will continue in the future, but under Fascism the re-distribution of labour will be controlled and proper arrangements will be made for the transfer and training of workers. At present, this important task is left practically untouched, and there are towns in the industrial areas of Britain filled with unemployed who will never be able to regain employment in their old trades, and who never have the opportunity of looking for work elsewhere.

Rationalisation, and the greater application of science to production, will mean in the future, as it has done in the past, considerably less demand for labour to produce a given quantity of goods. Nevertheless, such improvement in the technique of production must go on, and Fascism insists that whenever labour is displaced, either temporarily or per manently, it must not be thrown on to the scrap-heap. In the past, whenever industry has been rationalised or new machinery and new methods have been introduced, no regard has been paid to the human element, the men being regarded as industrial fodder. Fascism declares that where-ever labour is displaced, labour must not suffer.

There are strong humanitarian reasons why this should be so, for machinery was made to serve man and not to dominate it. But even regarding it from the point of view of efficiency, is it good business to allow human labour to deteriorate? Would any employer owning machinery allow it to fall into disrepair and to rust, just because he had no immediate use for it? No employer, of course, would treat machinery thus. Why should he be permitted to treat human beings as though they were less important?

Therefore, on the two grounds, humanitarian—which Fascists stress as of first importance—and secondly, on the ground of efficiency, Fascists declare that the human element in industry is valuable, and under no circumstances should it be allowed to degenerate when it is not in use.

WORK—NOT MAINTENANCE!

Therefore, Fascists vary the cry of Work or Maintenance, the great slogan of Keir Hardie. When men cannot be provided with work, then they are entitled to maintenance, but the first essential is the provision of work.

This brings up the point of alleged malingerers and work-shies. The number of men and women who prefer to live on the "dole," as it is miscalled, or on the receipts from the Public Assistance Committee, is not so large as some people imagine, but there is a small minority who have been driven to accept unemployment as inevitable, and have lost the desire to work.

How can Fascism distinguish the genuine seeker of work from the man or woman who is determined to avoid work? The test is simple. Make him an offer of work.

The principle of "work or starve" goes hand in hand with that of "work, not maintenance." If there are not jobs for everybody to go round, so that this test can be put into operation, then the principle of rationing" work can be applied. Here again the workers have given an admirable lead, for already in some parts of the country, they have commenced to put the principle into operation. In various parts of the coalfields of the North East of England, miners have, of their own initiative adopted a scheme whereby all should have three weeks work out of four, instead of three-quarters of the men being wholly employed and the other quarter totally unemployed.

Fascism agrees with such a principle, will extend it so that it covers the whole army of labour, but they will make this addition, that during the period when the labour is not required, it shall be adequately maintained.

No Means Test

Such a system is, of course, a great advance on the iniquitous system known as "the means test," by which the thrift of an individual and the thrift of his relatives, is severely penalised. The only test that should be applied is whether a man is willing to work, and this can only be done by offering him a job of work to do. Fascism, however, will go even further, and will create a Labour Reserve Fund out of the profits of industry to be set apart to assist workers who are displaced by schemes of rationalisation. Often such workers must incur special expenses, such as removing to another part of the country, or require training for a new industry. This Fund will meet such special expenditure.

The Labour Exchanges, too, will play a greater part in helping displaced workers to be re-absorbed into industry. Very few of the best jobs in industry are now filled through the Exchanges, but under Fascism regime these organisations will fulfil their original intention of finding work for displaced workers, instead of being as they are now, institutions at which the unemployed are badgered by harassed officials, whose success is judged by their ability to keep men and women from drawing benefits.

Particularly, too, will the British Union of Fascists turn its attention to the question of hours of labour. Many workers especially those in shops, are now expected to work abnormally long hours without extra remuneration. This would be made illegal and stern measures would be adopted to repress such practices.

No Strikes or Lockouts

Under Fascism, strikes and lockouts will not occur. Today employers, beset by a cruel financial policy and seeing their markets being stolen by foreign employers, using the cheapest labour, are compelled to indulge in "lockouts," in order to try to reduce wages. Workers, fighting against the tendency to reduce wages, and when they see employers prospering, fighting for a share of that prosperity, resort to the strike weapon. No employer or employee, however, sincerely believes that a lockout or a strike is a satisfactory method of solving a problem. Under Fascism, we claim that there would be no depression, and that as industry prospered, the workers would be certain, by the machinery of the Corporate State, to achieve a fair and satisfactory share of that prosperity. The economic causes of strikes and lockouts, therefore, would not exist under Fascism.

Increased Status

The trade union movement in the past has been divided in its tactics. At one period it has concentrated on its industrial side, attempting to make itself one hundred per cent strong, and, whenever it could, perfecting its organisation; at other periods, particularly after it had been beaten in an industrial struggle, it sought greater strength in the political field, endeavouring to increase its representation in Parliament and City and Town Councils.

The political weapon and the industrial weapon have been used alternatively, but Fascism ends this shooting off at two angles by uniting industrial aim and political aim. The Unions will be, within the Corporate State, an integral part of industry and government, carrying heavy responsibilities and duties both to government and workers.

This increased status of the trade union movement will call for a new type of leadership. The trade union leaders will have to concentrate on their job, and will have to perform it efficiently. They will be subject to criticism from the rank and file of members, who will still continue to have the power of appointment, but in addition, they will be subject to criticism from above.

The Corporate State will enable trade union leaders to function within industry to an extent they have never hitherto dreamed of, but it will demand from them a higher state of efficiency, and a completely disinterested devotion to the service of workers and the nation. Leaders will no longer be allowed to fatten on the pennies and shillings of the members of the unions, and neither will they be able to use the movement for social advancement.

Lastly, Fascists declare that the British worker must be protected from the foreign capitalist. The British trade union movement in the past has been hampered by its allegiance to the Free Trade philosophy. This, to some extent, was understandable. Trade union leaders did not care to give British employers a sheltered market by keeping out the foreign goods, because they knew that the British manufacturers would take an unfair advantage of the consumer.

Nevertheless, permitting the import of foreign goods made

by workers living on a low standard, was an illogical attitude for British trade unionists to take.

The British trade unionist would not permit goods to be turned out in this country by "blackleg" labour, yet they allowed goods turned out by similar labour to be sold in the home market, thereby throwing British workers out of jobs. Fascism recognises the dilemma of the trade unionist and puts forward a solution. The products of this foreign labour will not be permitted to enter the country, and it will be an essential part of the Corporate State machinery to see that the British manufacturer is not able to exploit either the worker or the consumer. This machinery is the keynote of our policy, for Fascism realises that the workers of Britain have to be protected from the unscrupulous home employer as well as the unscrupulous foreign employer, and also from the importer who does not care much where the goods come from so long as he can make a profit.

Fascism is the greatest crusade that has ever been under taken. It is not aimed at the working classes, it is not aimed against any class, it is aimed against evil—the evil of poverty, of waste and muddle, it is aimed at the creation of a world as a place fit for the twentieth century man and woman.

It has no enemies excepting poverty, misery, misrule and muddle. The world today is not good enough for the new spirit that is within us. Workers, therefore, have nothing to fear from Fascism. It stands for everything that they have stood for in the past and comes to their aid in the struggle against the rule of the selfish individual.

9 - Fascism Will Mean Peace

Fascism, lastly, will mean peace. Wars, it is said, are caused by "nationalism," that is, love of country. This is an illusion. Wars, in nearly every instance in modern times, have been caused by economic factors and the exploitation of the national spirit to further individual ends.

The causes of war are to be found in the conflicting interests and jealousies existing between powerful financial organisations. Financiers secure power in their own country by placing within the government "statesmen" who will do their bidding, and when the clash comes, they stimulate in peoples every crude instinct of hate and murder.

"Trade," it is said, "follows the flag." The reverse is the case. Trade has gone forth in the past, seeking profits for those sitting in the capitals of the country. When these traders, and their financiers, have found themselves in difficulties with traders and financiers in other nations they have not hesitated to use the "flag" as a cloak for their own misdemeanours. The "flag" is too sacred to British people all over the world to be mixed up with the sordidness of trade and finance. Let it fly freely over a people imbued with the spirit of service and duty, and above all, let it be kept out of the dust of the market place where it will be contaminated with the bargaining of the merchants and the usury of the financiers.

Fascism will end the system of scrambling for markets and for control of raw materials, for it believes in order and organisation in world trade, in the regulated exchange of commodities between country and country, according to a definite plan, instead of the present competitive basis that sets one continent against another, and country against country.

The world, it should not be forgotten, must ultimately be economically organised. Although this appears to stress the obvious, the fact today is that the world is something like sixty economic units. There are about sixty nations, all of whom regard themselves as a unit. If each was trying to keep itself separate from the others, perhaps no serious harm would result, but instead of following this policy, they are all interfering with each other. They are all desirous of expanding their markets, and adopt every device possible to under-sell their rivals, creating jealousy and ill-will between the nations.

Therefore, in the name of sanity, Fascists argue that the nations of the world must cease behaving like quarrelsome little shopkeepers; must end economic warfare among themselves, as it inevitably leads to chaos and the impoverish ment of their own peoples, and ultimately to armed antagonism.

There is no practical reason why this should not be done. The only obstacle is that the nations have not yet learned the absolute necessity of taking such a step. There are signs, however, that the peoples of civilised lands are appreciating this necessity for world order, and they are creating Fascist organisations in all parts of the world.

The world trend of events is helping such Fascist organisations for the peoples are becoming tired of the failures of non-Fascist statesmen. They see wars on a large scale being threatened; they see economic disasters, millions of people starving for years, the inability of nations to adopt any other course except to pile up armaments, or to end economic hostility. All around them they see the old order crumbling, while older statesmen are unable to grapple with a worsening world situation. These events are compelling both statesmen and peoples to become Fascist-minded.

Britain First

In the meantime, Fascists in Britain have a duty to perform here and now. There is no time to wait for the world-conversion to Fascism. We have to put Britain in order first. If we cannot settle our economic troubles here, then we cannot play our part in the effort to settle world troubles. While we are doing this, here, Fascists will be doing the same in other countries. Then, the time will be ripe for creating a Fascist Grand Council for the British Empire, a Fascist Grand Council for Europe and for the other Continents, until the whole world is under Fascist rule. Mankind is at the parting of the ways. We are moving either towards world collapse, or to world order. There is no standing still. Either we go backward or we go forward.

Fascism is in the direct line of social evolution. From free capitalism to controlled capitalism, from licence to duty, from conflict to co-operation. Fascism will win through the struggle; it is organised and disciplined; it possesses will-power and determination. It is our destiny.

Today, Fascists call upon the men and women of Britain to rouse themselves, to carry out the task before them; to create their future social and economic organisation— to eject chance and hazard from their lives and to build on a sure foundation, a Britain in which men and women will be strong mentally and physically, in which they will have the liberty to enjoy the richness of their own lives; in which strife between the nations will be no more, and war will exist only in the books of history.

Blackshirts dedicate their lives to this New Order that they themselves will create.

Lightning Source UK Ltd.
Milton Keynes UK
UKOW02f0126100315

9 781908 476678